I'm 60

Life at 60 in just 100 pages of wisdom

Volume III "The Life Collection"

Stefano Tosti

Contents

Presentation

Intro by Luigi Ciabotti and Camille Benoit

"I'm 60, Life at 60 in just 100 pages of wisdom" by Stefano Tosti is an enlightening and thought-provoking work that invites readers to rediscover meaning and passion in life before and after turning sixty. This book stands out for its ability to transform a stage of life often considered a final destination into a new adventure of growth and self-discovery.

Throughout its pages, the book sensitively and profoundly explores the journey that awaits us beyond sixty an age that can be seen not as an end, but as an open door to new opportunities. With engaging and reflective prose, the author guides the reader through the challenges and joys of this phase of life, offering concrete and inspiring tools to approach it with renewed enthusiasm.

The book covers a wide range of topics, from reflections on personal meaning and the discovery of new passions to practical strategies for enhancing physical, mental, and emotional well-being. With chapters dedicated to building new friendships, managing stress, and finding spiritual purpose, Tosti encourages us to live each day with intention and awareness.

One of the most captivating aspects of "I'm 60" is its holistic and inclusive approach. The author not only addresses the importance of health and personal growth but also explores how sharing experiences and engaging in online communities can enrich our lives. Through inspiring stories, the book provides readers with the keys to open new doors and discover inner riches previously unexpressed.

In this book, Stefano Tosti offers not just a guide, but a genuine call to action to embrace the future with optimism and joy. It is an invitation to celebrate every moment of life and to leave a lasting impact, a testament to how every stage of our existence can be lived with passion and meaning.

"I'm 60" is more than just a book; it is a celebration of life, an invitation to rediscover and reignite our vitality, and to live each day with a renewed sense of purpose. With elegant prose and profound wisdom, Stefano Tosti leads us toward a bright future full of possibilities, making this an essential read for anyone ready to explore and embrace the best that life has to offer after sixty.

Author's Dedication

I want to dedicate this book to all my friends and to all the people I have met throughout my life, across dozens of countries and hundreds of cities. Many of them have given me so much, and part of this book has been shaped by their advice and thoughts. The inspiration and willpower needed to put the first word of this book on my notebook were bestowed upon me by my mother Nilla.

Chapter 1: Embracing Change

Understanding the Journey of Aging

Understanding the journey of aging is a profound exploration that invites us to reflect on the intricacies of life as we transition into our later years. Aging is often perceived through a lens of loss or limitation, but it can also be viewed as a beautiful unfolding of opportunities for growth, wisdom, and renewed purpose. Embracing this journey means recognizing the rich tapestry of experiences that shape who we are and the potential that lies ahead. As we navigate this phase of life, it becomes vital to acknowledge the unique gifts that aging brings, allowing us to approach each day with a renewed sense of curiosity and hope.

Throughout our lives, we accumulate a wealth of experiences that contribute to our understanding of the world and ourselves. Each decade brings its own challenges and triumphs, and as we age, we gain insights that can empower us to redefine our narratives. This process of reflection can lead to moments of clarity about what truly matters to us, igniting passions long thought dormant. By engaging in life coaching and wellness practices, we can cultivate a deeper awareness of our strengths and desires, helping us transition from a life of mere existence to one filled with purpose and meaning.

Mindfulness plays a crucial role in this journey. As we age, it becomes increasingly important to cultivate an awareness of the present moment, allowing us to savor the richness of life rather than dwelling on the past or fearing the future. Mindfulness and stress management techniques can help us navigate the complexities of aging with grace and resilience. By learning to be fully present, we can appreciate the beauty in everyday moments, fostering a sense of gratitude that uplifts our spirits and enhances our overall well-being.

Confidence and self-esteem often fluctuate as we grow older, influenced by societal perceptions and personal experiences. However, it is essential to recognize that our value does not diminish with age; rather, it evolves. Embracing spiritual life coaching can guide us in rediscovering our inner strength and nurturing a positive self-image. By reframing our beliefs and focusing on self-compassion, we can build a foundation of confidence that empowers us to pursue new passions and forge meaningful connections with others.

Ultimately, understanding the journey of aging is about embracing the possibilities that lie ahead. It is an invitation to explore new interests, cultivate relationships, and discover the deeper meanings of our lives. By approaching this chapter with an open heart and a willingness to reflect, we can unlock the potential for joy, fulfillment, and purpose. Each day presents a new canvas, waiting for us to paint our stories with the colors of our experiences, passions, and dreams. If someone is asking when is the good time to embrace this mindset, answer is immediate and firm: of course, now!... Because it's good for anyone at any age. Let us embark on this journey together, celebrating the richness of our lives and the endless opportunities for growth that await us.

The Importance of Self-Reflection

Self-reflection is a powerful tool that can significantly enhance the quality of life for those over sixty. As we age, the experiences we accumulate often lead us to a crossroads where we seek deeper meaning and understanding of our journey. This process of looking inward allows us to assess our past, acknowledge our achievements, and come to terms with any unresolved issues. Engaging in self-reflection not only fosters personal growth but also ignites a newfound sense of purpose and passion that can enrich our later years.

In the realm of wellness and health coaching, self-reflection plays a vital role in promoting holistic well-being. By taking the time to examine our thoughts and feelings, we can identify patterns that may hinder our physical and mental health. This introspective practice encourages us to evaluate our lifestyle choices, habits, and emotional responses. With a clearer understanding of ourselves, we can make more informed decisions about our health and well-being, leading to a more balanced and fulfilling life.

Confidence and self-esteem often wane as we age, especially when we face the challenges of retirement, health issues, or the loss of loved ones. Self-reflection provides an opportunity to reconnect with our strengths and capabilities. By celebrating our accomplishments and recognizing our resilience, we can rebuild our sense of self-worth. This renewed confidence empowers us to pursue new interests, engage in social activities, and cultivate relationships, reminding us that our value is not diminished by age but rather enriched by the wisdom we have gained.

Mindfulness and stress management coaching greatly benefit from the practice of self-reflection. In moments of quiet contemplation, we can identify the sources of stress in our lives and develop strategies to cope with them. This mindfulness allows us to be present in each moment, appreciating the beauty of life's simple pleasures. Through self-reflection, we learn to let go of regrets and worries, fostering a sense of peace and acceptance. This stress reduction is essential for maintaining both mental and physical health as we navigate the complexities of aging.

Finally, self-reflection is a spiritual journey that invites us to explore our beliefs, values, and the legacy we wish to leave behind. As we ponder the meaning of our lives, we can connect with our inner selves and the greater universe. This exploration often leads to a deeper understanding of our purpose and the passions we wish to pursue. By embracing self-reflection, we not only honor our past but also pave the way for a vibrant future filled with intention and joy. Embrace this opportunity for growth, and let your journey of self-discovery illuminate the path ahead.

Setting the Stage for Discovery

Setting the stage for discovery is an essential part of embarking on a journey toward meaning and passion, especially after reaching the milestone of sixty years. This phase of life offers a unique opportunity for reflection, growth, and renewal. As we age, we often find ourselves reassessing our life experiences, values, and aspirations. This subchapter aims to guide you through the process of creating a nurturing environment that fosters introspection, encourages exploration, and ultimately leads you to discover deeper layers of purpose and fulfillment.

The first step in setting the stage for discovery involves cultivating a mindset of openness. Embrace the idea that your past experiences, both triumphs and challenges, serve as valuable lessons that can inform your future. Allow yourself to reflect on these moments without judgment. Instead of viewing them as regrets, consider them stepping stones that have shaped your identity. This shift in perspective can ignite curiosity and a desire to explore new avenues of interest. Remember, every chapter of your life has contributed to who you are today, and now is the time to leverage that wisdom toward new discoveries.

Creating a supportive atmosphere is also vital for fostering self-exploration. Surround yourself with individuals who uplift and inspire you, whether it's through friendships, support groups, or life coaching sessions. Engaging with like-minded individuals can provide encouragement and a sense of community as you navigate this journey. Additionally, consider establishing a physical space for reflection—perhaps a cozy corner in your home where you can journal, meditate, or simply sit in quiet contemplation. This dedicated space can serve as a sanctuary for your thoughts, allowing you to delve deeper into your desires and aspirations.

Mindfulness practices play a crucial role in enhancing self-awareness as you embark on this path. Incorporating mindfulness techniques such as meditation, deep breathing, or gentle yoga can help center your thoughts and emotions. These practices encourage you to remain present, fostering an environment where insights can flourish. As you cultivate mindfulness, you may find that your intuition becomes more pronounced, guiding you toward what resonates with your soul. Embrace these moments of clarity as valuable signs on your journey to rediscovering purpose and passion.

Lastly, it's essential to approach this stage of life with a spirit of exploration rather than pressure. Allow yourself the freedom to experiment with different activities, hobbies, or volunteering opportunities that pique your interest. This is not about finding a definitive answer but rather about enjoying the process of discovery. Whether it's taking a painting class, joining a book club, or exploring spirituality, each experience can bring new insights and connections. Celebrate each small step you take, and remember that the journey itself can be just as enriching as the destination. By setting the stage for discovery, you open the door to a vibrant, fulfilling chapter in your life.

Chapter 2: The Power of Mindfulness

Practicing Presence in Daily Life

Practicing presence in daily life is a vital skill that can enrich your experiences, foster deeper connections, and enhance your overall sense of well-being. As we age, the hustle and bustle of everyday life can sometimes lead us to overlook the beauty of the present moment. By consciously choosing to be present, you can cultivate a deeper appreciation for life, improve your mental clarity, and boost your emotional resilience. This practice is not just about slowing down; it's about engaging fully with each moment, no matter how mundane it may seem.

One effective way to begin practicing presence is through mindfulness exercises. These can be as simple as taking a few deep breaths before starting your day or setting aside a few minutes to observe your thoughts without judgment. Incorporating mindfulness into your daily routine can transform ordinary tasks into meaningful rituals. Whether you're enjoying a cup of tea, taking a walk, or even washing the dishes, try to immerse yourself fully in the experience. Notice the sensations, sounds, and sights around you. This practice not only grounds you in the moment but also helps to cultivate a sense of gratitude for the little things that often go unnoticed.

Another powerful method to enhance presence is through conscious listening. Many conversations are filled with distractions, but by actively engaging with what others are saying, you can create deeper connections. When speaking with friends or family, make it a point to focus solely on them. Put away your phone, make eye contact, and listen intently. This practice not only affirms the other person's importance but also enhances your own sense of belonging and connection. As you foster these meaningful interactions, you may find that your self-esteem and confidence grow, as you become more attuned to your relationships.

In addition to mindfulness and listening, consider integrating moments of reflection into your daily life. Taking a few moments to reflect on your day can help you recognize the richness of your experiences. Journaling is an excellent way to capture your thoughts and feelings, allowing you to process your experiences and gain insights into your personal journey. Reflecting on what brought you joy, what challenges you faced, and how you responded can deepen your self-awareness and clarify your passions. This practice not only enhances your sense of purpose but also encourages you to remain present in future moments.

Lastly, remember that practicing presence is a journey, not a destination. It requires patience and compassion for yourself. As you cultivate this skill, you may encounter moments of distraction or frustration, and that's perfectly normal. Embrace these moments as part of the process, and gently guide yourself back to the present. By making the conscious choice to practice presence in your daily life, you are opening the door to a more fulfilling and passionate existence. Celebrate each small victory along the way, and watch as the world around you become richer, more vibrant, and filled with purpose.

Techniques for Stress Reduction

Techniques for stress reduction can be a transformative aspect of life, especially as we navigate the complexities that come with aging. At this stage, many individuals find themselves reflecting on their lives, seeking meaning, and striving to cultivate a renewed sense of purpose. By incorporating effective stress reduction techniques, you can enhance your overall well-being, allowing you to embrace each day with vitality and joy.

One powerful technique for stress reduction is the practice of mindfulness. This involves focusing on the present moment and cultivating an attitude of acceptance towards your thoughts and feelings. Simple practices, such as mindful breathing or guided meditation, can be incredibly beneficial. Set aside a few minutes each day to sit quietly, close your eyes, and take deep, slow breaths. As you inhale and exhale, allow any worries and distractions to drift away. Mindfulness not only calms the mind but also helps you develop a deeper connection to yourself, fostering a sense of inner peace that can be invaluable in your journey of self-discovery.

Physical activity is another essential technique for reducing stress and boosting overall health. Engaging in regular exercise can release endorphins, which are natural mood lifters. Whether it's a gentle walk in the park, yoga, or dancing, find an activity that you enjoy and make it a part of your routine. Group classes can also provide a social element, allowing you to connect with others who share similar interests. This not only enhances your physical health but also nurtures your emotional well-being, reinforcing a sense of belonging and community.

In addition to mindfulness and physical activity, nurturing your spiritual side can be an incredible source of comfort and strength. Explore practices such as journaling, prayer, or connecting with nature. Reflecting on your life's journey and the lessons learned can provide clarity and insight, helping you to uncover your passions and purpose. Consider setting aside time each week to engage in spiritual exploration, whether through reading, attending community gatherings, or simply enjoying a quiet moment outdoors. This can foster a deeper sense of connection to something greater than yourself, empowering you to face challenges with resilience.

Lastly, don't underestimate the power of social connections in stress reduction. Building and maintaining relationships with family, friends, and community members can provide emotional support and companionship. Consider joining clubs, volunteering, or participating in local events that align with your interests. Sharing experiences and laughter with others can significantly alleviate stress and create a sense of fulfillment. Remember, it's never too late to forge new friendships or strengthen existing ones; these connections can enrich your life and contribute to a lasting sense of happiness and purpose.

By integrating these techniques into your daily life, you can cultivate a more balanced and fulfilling existence. Embrace the journey of self-discovery with an open heart, and allow these practices to guide you toward a life filled with meaning and passion. Each step you take towards reducing stress not only enhances your well-being but also empowers you to live your best life in this enriching chapter of your journey.

Building Inner Peace

Building inner peace is a journey that unfolds uniquely for each individual, especially as we navigate the later stages of our lives. At this age, we may find ourselves reflecting on past experiences, relationships, and the impact we've made on the world. However, the quest for inner tranquility can often feel overshadowed by regrets or unfulfilled dreams. This chapter aims to guide you through the process of cultivating a sense of calm and purpose, encouraging you to embrace the beauty of your current stage in life.

One of the most effective ways to nurture inner peace is through mindfulness. Practicing mindfulness allows us to focus on the present moment, reducing the mental clutter that often leads to stress and anxiety. Simple techniques such as deep breathing, meditation, or even mindful walking can help ground you in the now. As you become more aware of your thoughts and feelings without judgment, you'll discover a newfound clarity that empowers you to let go of past burdens and embrace the present with an open heart.

Incorporating wellness practices into your daily routine is another powerful way to cultivate inner peace. Engaging in regular physical activity, nurturing a balanced diet, and ensuring adequate rest can significantly improve your mental and emotional state. As you prioritize your health, you'll create a stronger foundation for self-esteem and confidence. Remember, it's never too late to embark on a journey of self-care; even small changes can lead to profound transformations, helping you to feel more centered and at peace with yourself.

Furthermore, exploring your spirituality can be a profound avenue for building inner peace. Whether you find solace in nature, prayer, or connecting with a community, spirituality can provide a sense of belonging and purpose. Reflecting on your values and what brings you joy can foster a deeper understanding of your life's meaning. This exploration allows you to align your daily actions with your spiritual beliefs, creating harmony within yourself and enhancing your overall well-being.

Lastly, embrace the art of gratitude as a means to foster inner peace. Taking time each day to reflect on what you are grateful for shifts your focus from what is lacking to the abundance that already exists in your life. Keeping a gratitude journal can be a simple yet effective practice, allowing you to document your thoughts and feelings. As you cultivate an attitude of gratitude, you'll find that it not only enriches your own life but also positively impacts those around you, creating a ripple effect of peace and joy in your community. Building inner peace is not merely a destination; it's an ongoing journey that invites you to appreciate every moment and to live with intention and passion.

Chapter 3: Reconnecting with Yourself

Identifying Core Values

Identifying core values is a transformative journey that can lead to deeper self-understanding and fulfillment, especially for those of us who have gathered a wealth of experience over the years. As we age, it's natural to reflect on our lives, considering what truly matters to us. This process can be especially enriching after the age of 60, as it allows us to sift through the layers of our experiences and uncover the principles that have guided us. By identifying these core values, we can connect more meaningfully with ourselves and others, enriching our lives and the lives of those around us.

To begin this journey, set aside some quiet time for introspection. Find a comfortable space where you won't be disturbed. Consider the moments in your life when you felt most fulfilled, joyful, or proud. What were you doing at those times? Who were you with? Reflect on these experiences and jot down themes that emerge. You might discover that values such as family, kindness, adventure, or creativity resonate strongly with you. This exercise can illuminate patterns in your life and help you recognize the beliefs that have shaped your decisions and actions.

Another effective way to identify your core values is to think about the qualities you admire in others. Who do you look up to, and what traits do they embody? This admiration can be a window into your own values. For instance, if you deeply respect someone for their integrity, it may indicate that honesty is a core value for you. By understanding what you appreciate in others, you can gain insight into the principles that you hold dear and wish to embody in your own life.

Once you have a clearer idea of your core values, consider how they manifest in your daily life. Are there areas where you feel misaligned with these values? Perhaps you value health and wellness but find yourself neglecting your physical well-being. Recognizing these discrepancies can motivate you to make positive changes, leading to a more authentic and fulfilling life. Embrace this opportunity to realign your actions with your values, allowing for a more purposeful existence that honors what is truly important to you.

As you continue to explore and embrace your core values, remember that this journey is not just about self-discovery; it's also about connection. Sharing your values with loved ones and engaging in conversations about what matters most to you can deepen your relationships. Additionally, this clarity can guide you in making decisions that enhance your well-being and cultivate your passions. Embrace this transformative process, knowing that identifying your core values is a significant step toward living a life filled with meaning, joy, and renewed purpose.

Exploring Passions and Interests

Exploring passions and interests is a vital journey at any stage of life, but it holds particular significance for those over 60. This period is often seen as a time of reflection and reevaluation, where individuals can embrace the freedom to pursue what truly brings them joy. As we age, the societal pressures and obligations that once dictated our choices begin to fade. This newfound clarity presents an opportunity to delve into hobbies, interests, and passions that may have been set aside during the busyness of earlier years. By reconnecting with these elements, one can foster a sense of purpose and fulfillment that enriches the later stages of life.

Engaging in activities that ignite passion is not just about personal enjoyment; it also serves as a powerful tool for enhancing overall well-being. Research shows that pursuing interests can improve mental health, boost self-esteem, and reduce stress levels. Whether it's painting, gardening, writing, or learning a new instrument, each pursuit offers a unique way to express oneself and cultivate creativity. In this chapter, we will explore how to identify these passions, assess their relevance in our lives, and integrate them into our daily routines. This process can be both liberating and empowering, allowing individuals to reclaim their identities beyond the roles they have played in the past.

Mindfulness plays a significant role in this exploration. By practicing mindfulness, individuals can become more aware of their thoughts and feelings, helping to illuminate what truly excites and motivates them. Taking the time to reflect on past experiences can reveal forgotten joys and interests. Perhaps there's a long-lost love for painting or a curiosity about photography that was never fully explored. By cultivating mindfulness, seniors can enhance their ability to listen to their inner selves, leading them to passions that resonate deeply with their current life stage.

Life coaching can be an invaluable resource in this journey. A skilled coach can provide guidance and support, helping individuals sift through their experiences and identify what brings them joy. The coaching process encourages self-discovery and accountability, making it easier to take actionable steps toward pursuing interests. By setting achievable goals, such as joining a local art class or starting a book club, individuals can gradually integrate their passions into their lives, fostering a sense of accomplishment and connection with others.

Ultimately, exploring passions and interests is about more than just filling time; it's about creating a rich tapestry of experiences that contribute to a meaningful life. As individuals embrace their passions, they not only enhance their own well-being but also inspire those around them. This journey can lead to newfound friendships, opportunities for learning, and a deeper connection to one's own spirit. As we navigate the path of purpose and passion discovery, let us encourage one another to remain curious and open-hearted, allowing the richness of our interests to illuminate the beautiful chapter of life that comes after 60.

Journaling for Clarity

In the journey of self-discovery, particularly after the age of sixty, journaling can serve as a powerful tool for clarity and reflection. This practice offers a safe space to explore thoughts, emotions, and experiences that shape our lives. As we age, the accumulation of memories and lessons can sometimes feel overwhelming. Journaling allows us to sift through this mental clutter, helping us identify patterns, recognize our feelings, and gain insight into what truly matters to us. By putting pen to paper, we can articulate our innermost thoughts, leading to a deeper understanding of ourselves.

For those navigating the complexities of life after 60, journaling can enhance wellness and mental health. Engaging in this reflective practice has been shown to reduce stress, promote mindfulness, and improve emotional regulation. Each page turned offers an opportunity to pause and breathe, allowing us to process our experiences without judgment. Through writing, we can articulate our fears, hopes, and dreams, transforming them into tangible words. This process not only alleviates anxiety but also fosters a sense of accomplishment and empowerment, reminding us that our voices and stories matter.

Moreover, journaling can be a pathway to rediscovering purpose and passion in our lives. As we reflect on our past experiences, we may uncover interests or aspirations that had been set aside. Writing about what brings us joy or fulfillment can reignite a sense of enthusiasm and inspire new pursuits. Whether it's exploring a long-forgotten hobby or engaging in volunteer work, journaling helps clarify what we want to achieve in this new chapter of life. It encourages us to dream again and to set intentions for a fulfilling future.

Incorporating journaling into a daily routine doesn't have to be daunting. Start with just a few minutes each day, allowing your thoughts to flow freely without the pressure of structure or grammar. You might find it helpful to use prompts such as "What made me smile today?" or "What challenges did I overcome this week?" These questions can guide your reflection and help you focus on the positive aspects of your life. Over time, you'll likely notice how your insights evolve, shaping a clearer vision of your path forward.

Ultimately, journaling is a deeply personal journey that can lead to profound clarity and self-discovery. By embracing this practice, you open the door to understanding your emotions, aspirations, and values. As you navigate the complexities of life after sixty, remember that each entry in your journal is a step towards greater awareness and fulfillment. Trust the process, and allow yourself the grace to explore the depths of your heart and mind. In doing so, you will not only find clarity but also a renewed sense of purpose and passion for the life that lies ahead.

Chapter 4: Cultivating Conf and Self-Esteem

Overcoming Limiting Beliefs

Overcoming limiting beliefs is a pivotal step in the journey of self-discovery, especially as we embrace the later chapters of our lives. Many individuals over the age of 60 may find themselves grappling with thoughts that restrict their potential, whispering doubts that suggest it's too late to pursue dreams or embark on new adventures. Yet, recognizing that these beliefs are not truths, but rather the echoes of past experiences and societal expectations, is the first stride towards liberation. By challenging these narratives, we can open ourselves up to a world brimming with possibilities, allowing us to redefine what aging means and how joyfully we can live it.

The first step in overcoming limiting beliefs involves awareness. Take a moment to reflect on the thoughts that arise when you contemplate change or new experiences. Do you find yourself saying, "I'm too old for that," or "I could never do that"? Acknowledging these thoughts is crucial, as they often stem from fear and uncertainty rather than reality. By recognizing them, you create space for a more positive dialogue.

Consider journaling about these beliefs; writing them down can help you examine their validity and begin the process of reframing them into something more empowering. This practice not only fosters self-awareness but also acts as a powerful tool for personal growth.

Next, it's important to challenge these beliefs actively. Ask yourself where they originated and whether they still serve you. Many of our limiting beliefs are rooted in the past, shaped by experiences or messages we received from others. As you reflect on these origins, remind yourself that you are not defined by a single moment in time. Embrace the idea that growth is a lifelong journey and that your capacity for learning and change remains intact, regardless of age. Surrounding yourself with supportive and encouraging individuals—whether through life coaching or wellness groups—can help reinforce this new mindset, providing you with the encouragement needed to step outside of your comfort zone.

Practicing mindfulness can also play a significant role in overcoming limiting beliefs. By cultivating a habit of present-moment awareness, you can observe your thoughts without judgment, allowing you to detach from negative self-talk. Mindfulness encourages acceptance and compassion towards oneself, fostering a sense of peace that can diminish the power of limiting beliefs. Engage in mindfulness exercises, such as meditation or deep breathing, to help center your thoughts and create a clearer perspective. As you become more attuned to your inner dialogue, you can consciously replace discouraging thoughts with affirmations of your capabilities and worth.

Finally, embracing a spirit of curiosity can transform the way you approach life after 60. Instead of viewing limitations as barriers, reframe them as opportunities for exploration. This shift in perspective can ignite a renewed sense of passion and purpose, encouraging you to pursue interests that resonate with your heart. Whether it's picking up a new hobby, volunteering, or traveling to a place you've always wanted to visit, each step taken outside your comfort zone can chip away at the limitations you've placed on yourself. Remember, the journey of self-discovery does not have an expiration date; it is an ongoing adventure that can lead to profound fulfillment and joy. By overcoming limiting beliefs, you can fully embrace the richness of life that awaits you.

Celebrating Life Experiences and Achievements

Celebrating life experiences and achievements is an essential aspect of embracing the journey we take as we age. After 60, many individuals find themselves reflecting on their past, often with a mix of nostalgia and gratitude. It is crucial to honor these experiences, not just as memories but as significant milestones that shape who we are today. Each achievement, big or small, contributes to our personal narrative, reminding us of our resilience and capacity for growth. By celebrating these moments, we reinforce our sense of identity and purpose, paving the way for new chapters in our lives.

As we delve into the heart of our past, it becomes evident that every experience holds value. Whether it was a career triumph, raising a family, or pursuing a long-held passion, each achievement reflects our unique journey. Taking the time to acknowledge and celebrate these moments serves as a powerful reminder of our capabilities. It cultivates self-esteem and confidence, encouraging us to continue seeking new challenges and opportunities that align with our passions. By recognizing what we have accomplished, we not only honor our past but also inspire ourselves to pursue new adventures.

Engaging in mindfulness and reflection can deeply enhance the experience of celebrating our achievements. Mindfulness invites us to be present, allowing us to savor the feelings of joy and satisfaction that arise when we think of our successes. This practice helps us shift away from any negative self-talk and instead focus on gratitude. By creating rituals—perhaps through journaling, sharing stories with loved ones, or even hosting a celebration—we can elevate our reflections into meaningful experiences. These practices not only foster a sense of community but also reinforce our connection to the present, making our achievements feel vibrant and alive.

Moreover, as we reflect on our journeys, it's vital to remember the lessons learned along the way. Challenges often accompany our achievements, molding us into more resilient individuals. Acknowledging these hurdles not only empowers us but also provides a roadmap for others who may be facing similar struggles. Sharing our stories can inspire those around us, creating a ripple effect of encouragement and empowerment. By celebrating our life experiences, we not only honor ourselves but also become beacons of hope for others navigating their own paths.

In this stage of life, we have the opportunity to redefine what success means to us. It is not solely about accolades or recognition; rather, it encompasses the fulfillment of pursuing our passions and the joy of personal growth. Celebrating life experiences and achievements invites us to embrace our journey wholeheartedly. As we reflect, let us do so with an open heart, cherishing the past while looking forward to the endless possibilities ahead. Remember, every moment is worth celebrating, and each day holds the potential for new achievements that align with our purpose and passion.

Building a Supportive Community

Building a supportive community is a crucial aspect of enhancing the quality of life, especially as we transition into our golden years. For many elderly individuals, the sense of isolation can be overwhelming. However, establishing connections with like-minded individuals can foster a sense of belonging and purpose. A supportive community can serve as a sanctuary, where individuals share experiences, challenges, and triumphs, ultimately leading to deeper relationships and collective growth. As you embark on this journey of self-discovery and fulfillment, remember that the connections you build can significantly enhance your emotional and spiritual well-being.

Engaging with others who share your interests and values can create a nurturing environment that promotes wellness and health. Joining local clubs, spiritual groups, or wellness workshops can provide not only companionship but also opportunities for learning and personal development. These gatherings can be sources of inspiration, where members motivate each other to embrace healthier lifestyles, explore new hobbies, and pursue dreams that may have been set aside. The energy and enthusiasm of a supportive group can reignite your passion for life, encouraging you to set and achieve personal goals that resonate with your true self.

Confidence and self-esteem often flourish in a supportive community. When surrounded by individuals who uplift and encourage one another, it becomes easier to challenge self-doubt and negative beliefs. Celebrating each other's achievements, no matter how small, reinforces a positive self-image. Engaging in group activities that emphasize collaboration rather than competition can create a safe space for self-expression and personal growth. As you share your stories and listen to others, you will find that vulnerability can lead to strength, fostering deeper connections and a greater sense of self-worth.

Mindfulness and stress management are vital components of a fulfilling life, especially in later years. A supportive community can provide a platform for practicing mindfulness together, whether through mediation sessions, yoga classes, or simply sharing moments of gratitude. These practices not only help in alleviating stress but also cultivate an awareness of the present moment, enhancing your overall sense of peace. When you share these experiences with others, you create a collective energy that enriches the process, allowing each participant to grow in their mindfulness journey while being supported by their peers.

Finally, spiritual life coaching can flourish within a nurturing community. Engaging in discussions about purpose, spirituality, and personal beliefs can lead to profound insights and transformative experiences. A supportive group can help individuals explore their spiritual paths, encouraging open dialogue and shared exploration of life's deeper questions. This environment fosters a sense of connection to something greater, empowering participants to discover and embrace their unique purposes. In building a supportive community, you not only contribute to your own growth but also become a guiding light for others, creating a ripple effect of encouragement and inspiration in the lives around you.

Chapter 5: Spiritual Exploration

Defining Spirituality in Your Life

Defining spirituality in your life can be a deeply personal journey, one that invites you to explore your values, beliefs, and connections to something greater than yourself. As you navigate the later stages of life, this exploration becomes increasingly important. Spirituality is not confined to religious practices; it encompasses a broader understanding of your essence, purpose, and the relationships you nurture with others and the world around you. By taking the time to reflect on what spirituality means to you, you can cultivate a sense of peace, fulfillment, and direction, enriching your daily experiences.

At its core, spirituality is about understanding your place in the universe and finding meaning in your experiences. For many, this involves connecting with nature, engaging in creative pursuits, or fostering relationships that bring joy and a sense of belonging. As you reflect on your life, consider the moments that have felt most profound or transformative. These experiences often hold keys to understanding your personal spirituality. By recognizing these pivotal moments, you can begin to integrate them into your daily life, allowing them to guide your actions and decisions moving forward.

Mindfulness and self-awareness are essential components of spiritual exploration. Practicing mindfulness allows you to be present in each moment, fostering an appreciation for the beauty and complexity of life. This practice can help you identify what resonates with your spirit, whether it's a quiet morning ritual, a walk in the park, or engaging in meaningful conversations with loved ones. As you become more attuned to your inner self, you'll find that your confidence and self-esteem will naturally flourish, empowering you to embrace your unique path and purpose.

Engaging in spiritual life coaching can be a valuable resource as you work to define spirituality in your life. A coach can help you clarify your beliefs, set intentions, and develop practices that resonate with your core values. This support can be particularly beneficial as you face transitions, encouraging you to explore new perspectives and embrace change with confidence. Through guided reflection and conversation, you can uncover insights that lead to a deeper understanding of your spiritual identity and how it influences your daily life.

Ultimately, defining spirituality in your life is an ongoing process, one that evolves as you grow and change. Embrace this journey with an open heart and mind, recognizing that it is never too late to discover new passions and purposes. By consciously integrating spirituality into your life, you create a foundation for wellness, resilience, and joy. Remember, this exploration is not about reaching a final destination but rather about enjoying the journey itself, celebrating each step as you cultivate a richer, more meaningful existence.

Practices for Spiritual Growth

In the journey of life, particularly as we reach our later years, the pursuit of spiritual growth can be a profound source of meaning and fulfillment. Spiritual growth is not confined to any particular belief system; rather, it encompasses a broad spectrum of practices that foster a deep connection with oneself and the universe. Engaging in these practices can enhance your sense of purpose and passion, leading to a more enriched life. As you explore these avenues, remember that the path to spiritual growth is unique for each individual, and your experiences are valid and valuable.

One effective practice for spiritual growth is the art of mindfulness. Mindfulness invites you to immerse yourself in the present moment, fully experiencing your thoughts, feelings, and surroundings without judgment. This practice can be particularly beneficial for managing stress and enhancing overall well-being. Begin by dedicating just a few minutes each day to mindful breathing or gentle meditation. As you become more attuned to your inner self, you may find clarity and peace that helps you navigate the complexities of life. This awareness can also lead to greater confidence in your decisions and actions, allowing you to embrace your journey with renewed vigor.

Another powerful tool for spiritual growth is reflection. Taking time to reflect on your life experiences allows you to gain insights into your values, beliefs, and motivations. Consider keeping a journal where you can document your thoughts and feelings. Reflecting on past challenges and triumphs can reveal patterns and lessons that inform your current choices. This practice not only boosts self-esteem but also fosters resilience, enabling you to approach new experiences with an open heart and mind. Through reflection, you can connect with your inner wisdom and clarify your purpose, steering your life toward what truly matters to you.

Cultivating gratitude is a transformative practice that can significantly enhance your spiritual growth. By consciously acknowledging the blessings in your life, whether big or small, you shift your focus from what may be lacking to the abundance that surrounds you. Start a daily gratitude practice by listing three things you are thankful for each day. This simple act can elevate your mood and foster a sense of connection with others. As you recognize the beauty in everyday moments, you may find a deeper appreciation for life itself, reinforcing your sense of purpose and passion in this stage of your journey.

Finally, consider embracing community as a vital aspect of your spiritual growth. Engaging with others who share similar values and interests can provide support and inspiration. Whether through group meditation, book clubs, or volunteering opportunities, connecting with like-minded individuals fosters a sense of belonging and shared purpose. These interactions can enhance your self-esteem and confidence, reminding you that you are not alone on this path. By nurturing relationships and participating in communal activities, you enrich not only your own life but also the lives of those around you, creating a ripple effect of positivity and spiritual growth.

As you embark on or continue your journey of spiritual growth, remember that each step you take is significant. Embrace these practices with an open heart, and allow yourself the grace to explore what resonates with you. This period of life is an opportunity for deep reflection and exploration, where you can cultivate your unique sense of purpose and passion.

Finding Meaning in Everyday Moments

Finding meaning in everyday moments is an enriching journey that can transform the ordinary into the extraordinary, especially as we navigate the later chapters of our lives. Each day presents us with a tapestry of experiences, many of which we may overlook in our quest for larger milestones. However, it is often in these small, seemingly mundane moments that we can uncover significant insights about ourselves and what truly matters to us. By cultivating a mindset that seeks meaning in daily experiences, we open ourselves up to a deeper connection with life and a renewed sense of purpose.

As we age, the pace of life may slow down, providing us with the perfect opportunity to embrace mindfulness. This practice encourages us to be present and fully engaged in the now, allowing us to appreciate the beauty in simple tasks, such as sipping a cup of tea, watching the leaves dance in the wind, or sharing laughter with a friend. Mindfulness invites us to pause and reflect on our surroundings and feelings, transforming routine moments into opportunities for self-discovery and appreciation. By approaching life with curiosity and awareness, we can find joy and meaning in the simplest of actions.

Additionally, finding meaning in everyday moments can significantly enhance our overall well-being. Engaging in activities that resonate with our passions—be it gardening, painting, or volunteering—can foster a sense of fulfillment and connection. These moments serve as reminders of our strengths and interests, reinstating our self-esteem and reinforcing our sense of identity. By recognizing and engaging in what brings us joy, we not only enhance our quality of life but also inspire those around us to seek their own moments of meaning.

It's also essential to reflect on our relationships and the connections we maintain. Conversations with family, friends, or even a neighbor can become profound moments of shared understanding and love. Taking time to listen, share stories, or simply enjoy each other's company can nurture our spirits and remind us of our place in the world. These interactions often hold the key to finding deeper significance in our lives. By fostering these connections, we can enrich our emotional landscape and create a supportive network that celebrates the beauty of everyday experiences.

Ultimately, finding meaning in everyday moments is about embracing a life filled with intention and awareness. It encourages us to step back from the distractions that often cloud our vision and to focus on what truly matters. By incorporating practices such as gratitude, reflection, and mindfulness into our daily routines, we can cultivate a profound appreciation for life's little gifts. As we uncover the richness of our experiences, we discover that it is never too late to live with passion and purpose, transforming every day into a canvas for joy and meaning.

Chapter 6: Discovering Purpose

What Does Purpose Mean at This Stage?

What purpose means in this stage of life transcends mere achievement or productivity; it embodies a profound sense of fulfillment and connectivity. At sixty and beyond, many individuals find themselves reflecting on their past experiences and considering the legacy they wish to leave behind. This reflection can ignite a powerful journey toward discovering deeper meanings in their daily lives. Understanding purpose at this stage is about embracing who you are, acknowledging your life's journey, and recognizing the unique contributions you can still make to the world around you.

As we age, our perspectives often shift, allowing us to see value in different aspects of life. Purpose is no longer just tied to career milestones or external validation; it becomes more about the relationships we nurture, the wisdom we share, and the joy we cultivate. This transformative phase encourages individuals to explore passions that may have been sidelined during earlier years. Whether it's engaging in community service, pursuing creative interests, or simply spending quality time with loved ones, finding purpose in these areas can enrich your life and provide a renewed sense of belonging.

Wellness and health coaching play a crucial role in this discovery of purpose by helping individuals understand the importance of self-care. At this stage, caring for your physical, emotional, and mental health becomes essential for maintaining vitality and pursuing passions. By focusing on wellness, you equip yourself with the energy and resilience needed to explore new interests and engage meaningfully with others. This holistic approach encourages a balanced lifestyle that supports both your well-being and your quest for purpose, making it a vital part of your journey.

Confidence and self-esteem coaching can also be transformative as you redefine your purpose. Many individuals may feel apprehensive about pursuing new endeavors or rediscovering old passions, believing that they lack the skills or the opportunities to do so. However, building confidence at this stage is about recognizing your inherent worth and the rich experiences you bring to the table. Embracing your unique journey can empower you to take bold steps toward fulfilling your dreams, ultimately enhancing your sense of purpose and satisfaction in life.

Mindfulness and spiritual life coaching offer valuable tools for navigating this meaningful exploration. Mindfulness encourages present-moment awareness, allowing you to appreciate the beauty in everyday experiences and fostering a sense of gratitude. Spiritual life coaching, on the other hand, helps you connect with your core values and beliefs, guiding you toward a deeper understanding of your purpose. Together, these practices can cultivate clarity and insight, enabling you to approach this stage of life with an open heart and a curious mind, ready to embrace the possibilities that lie ahead.

Aligning Actions with Values

Aligning actions with values is a powerful practice that can bring clarity and satisfaction to life, especially in the later years. For individuals over 60, this alignment becomes increasingly significant as they reflect on their past experiences and consider their legacies. This subchapter invites you to explore the importance of understanding your core values and ensuring that your daily actions mirror these beliefs. When we act in accordance with what we truly value, we cultivate a sense of purpose that can enhance our overall well-being.

To begin this journey of alignment, take a moment to identify what truly matters to you. Consider the values that have shaped your life choices and relationships. These might include love, integrity, adventure, community, or personal growth. Creating a list of your top five values can serve as a guiding star for your decision-making process. When you have clarity about what you stand for, it becomes easier to make choices that resonate with your sense of self, leading to greater fulfillment and joy in your daily life.

As you reflect on your values, think about the actions you currently engage in. Are they in harmony with what you cherish most? It can be revealing to assess how your daily routines, social interactions, and even your leisure activities align with your values. If you find discrepancies, consider small, manageable changes that can help bridge the gap. For instance, if community service is a core value, you might explore local volunteering opportunities that resonate with your interests. Such actions not only align with your values but also foster connections and enhance your sense of belonging.

Mindfulness plays a crucial role in this alignment process. By practicing mindfulness, you can cultivate a deeper awareness of your thoughts and feelings, which helps you recognize when your actions diverge from your values. This heightened awareness empowers you to make conscious choices that reflect your true self. Incorporating mindfulness techniques, such as meditation or simple breathing exercises, can provide you with the clarity needed to evaluate your decisions and their alignment with your values.

Ultimately, aligning your actions with your values is a journey of self-discovery and growth. It encourages you to live authentically and purposefully, allowing you to leave a meaningful legacy. Embracing this alignment can lead to increased confidence, better mental health, and a profound sense of peace. As you navigate this new chapter of your life, remember that each step you take to align your actions with your values is a step toward a more passionate, purposeful existence. Embrace this journey with an open heart and mind, and watch how it transforms your experience of life after 60.

Creating a Personal Mission Statement

Creating a personal mission statement is a powerful exercise that can significantly enhance your sense of purpose and direction, especially in the later chapters of life. As you reflect on your experiences, values, and aspirations, crafting a mission statement can help clarify your intentions and serve as a guiding light for your decisions moving forward. Embracing this endeavor encourages you to articulate what truly matters to you, fostering a renewed sense of confidence and self-esteem as you navigate the opportunities that lie ahead.

Begin by taking the time to reflect on your life's journey. Consider the moments that brought you joy, the challenges you overcame, and the values that have shaped your identity. This introspective process can be incredibly liberating, allowing you to identify the core principles that resonate with you. Engage in mindfulness practices, such as journaling or meditative reflection, to ground yourself in the present moment. By doing so, you create a rich tapestry of insights that can inform your mission statement, empowering you to move forward with clarity and intention.

Once you have gathered your thoughts, start drafting your personal mission statement. Aim for a concise and meaningful expression of your purpose that captures your values and aspirations. It might include aspects of wellness, health, spirituality, or any passions that ignite your spirit. Remember, this statement is deeply personal and should reflect your unique journey. Allow your words to flow freely, and don't hesitate to revise and refine them until they resonate with your true self. This is a living document that can evolve as you grow, so embrace the process with openness and enthusiasm.

Sharing your mission statement with others can also be a powerful way to reinforce your commitment to it. Whether it's with family, friends, or a supportive community, discussing your mission can enhance your confidence and accountability. Engaging in dialogues around your aspirations can foster deeper connections and inspire those around you to embark on their own journeys of self-discovery. Remember, you are not alone on this path; many individuals seek to find meaning and clarity in their lives, and your experience can serve as a beacon of encouragement for others.

Finally, revisit your mission statement regularly. Life is dynamic, and your goals and aspirations may shift over time. By periodically reflecting on your mission, you can ensure it continues to align with your evolving sense of self and purpose. This practice of purposeful reflection will not only reinforce your commitment to living intentionally but also deepen your understanding of what brings you joy and fulfillment. Embrace this journey with an open heart, and allow your personal mission statement to guide you toward a vibrant and meaningful life in the years to come.

Chapter 7: Setting Intentions for the Future

Goal-Setting for Fulfillment

Goal-setting is a powerful tool that can significantly enhance fulfillment in the later stages of life. As we age, many of us find ourselves reflecting on our past achievements, dreams, and desires. This process of introspection can often bring clarity to what we truly want moving forward. Setting goals is not merely about ticking off boxes; it's about creating a roadmap for a more meaningful and passionate life. By identifying what truly matters to you, you can cultivate a sense of purpose that enriches your daily experiences.

The first step in effective goal-setting is to engage in self-reflection. Take the time to consider your values, interests, and aspirations. What brings you joy? What activities make you feel alive? This contemplation is essential because it aligns your goals with your innermost desires, ensuring that they resonate with who you are. Perhaps you've always wanted to explore a new hobby, volunteer in your community, or even write a memoir. Whatever it may be, recognizing these aspirations can ignite a fire within you, fueling a renewed sense of purpose.

Once you have identified your passions, it's time to translate them into actionable goals. Break down your larger aspirations into smaller, manageable steps. For instance, if your goal is to learn a new language, set specific milestones such as dedicating a certain number of minutes each day to practice or enrolling in a local class. This structured approach not only makes your goals more attainable but also keeps you motivated as you celebrate each small victory along the way. Remember, every step forward is a step toward fulfillment.

As you embark on this journey of goal-setting, it's vital to maintain a positive mindset. Embrace the idea that it's never too late to pursue your passions or to set new goals. Challenges may arise, but viewing them as opportunities for growth can make all the difference. Surround yourself with supportive friends, family, or even life coaches who can encourage you and provide accountability. Sharing your goals with others can create a powerful network of support, amplifying your motivation and confidence as you navigate this exciting phase of life.

Finally, integrate mindfulness into your goal-setting process. Take time to pause and reflect on your progress, celebrating both your achievements and the lessons learned along the way. Mindfulness allows you to stay present, helping you appreciate the journey rather than focusing solely on the destination. This approach fosters a deeper connection to your goals, transforming them from mere tasks into meaningful pursuits. By setting goals that resonate with your true self and approaching them with intention, you can cultivate a life filled with fulfillment, passion, and joy in your golden years.

Embracing New Opportunities

Embracing new opportunities is a transformative journey that begins with a shift in perspective. As we age, it's common to feel a sense of loss or nostalgia for what once was. However, this period of life also presents a unique chance to explore new paths, venture into uncharted territories, and reinvent ourselves. The key lies in recognizing that every new opportunity is not merely a challenge to face but a doorway to personal growth, fulfillment, and joy. By adopting a mindset that welcomes change, we open ourselves to experiences that can enrich our lives beyond our wildest dreams.

Life coaching can play a crucial role in this transition. A skilled coach helps individuals identify their strengths, passions, and values, guiding them to set realistic goals that align with their newfound aspirations. At sixty and beyond, many find themselves with newfound freedom—whether it's retirement, an empty nest, or a change in health status. This is the perfect time to reassess what brings joy and meaning to our lives. A life coach can provide the support needed to navigate these waters, helping you to embrace the opportunities that lie ahead with confidence and enthusiasm.

Wellness and health coaching are also vital components of embracing new opportunities. Physical health is intrinsically linked to our mental and emotional well-being. Engaging in a new exercise routine, trying out a healthy diet, or even exploring mindfulness practices can invigorate both body and spirit. As we prioritize our well-being, we create a solid foundation from which to explore new interests and hobbies. The energy and vitality gained from such practices can unleash creativity and passion, allowing us to approach life with renewed vigor and curiosity.

Building confidence and self-esteem is another essential aspect of seizing new opportunities. Many elderly individuals may struggle with self-doubt, feeling that they are too old to try new things or that they lack the skills necessary to succeed. However, confidence coaching can help dismantle these barriers. By celebrating small victories and recognizing the wealth of experience that life has provided, individuals can rediscover their ability to learn and grow. Embracing new opportunities becomes not only a possibility but an exciting venture that can lead to profound self-discovery and satisfaction.

Finally, spiritual and mindfulness coaching can be invaluable in this journey. Finding meaning and purpose often requires a deeper connection to ourselves and the world around us. Engaging in reflective practices such as meditation, journaling, or connecting with nature can open our hearts and minds to the possibilities that life holds. This deeper understanding can empower us to pursue our passions wholeheartedly, guiding us toward opportunities that resonate with our true selves. As we embrace these new chapters, we find that it is never too late to create a life filled with purpose, connection, and joy.

Overcoming Fear of Change

Overcoming the fear of change is a vital step toward embracing a more fulfilling life, especially for those of us over 60. As we navigate this stage of life, it's common to feel apprehensive about the unknown that change often brings. However, it's important to recognize that change is not something to be feared but rather an opportunity for growth and renewal. By shifting our perspective and cultivating an open mindset, we can transform fear into a powerful catalyst for positive transformation.

One of the most effective ways to overcome fear is to acknowledge and confront it. Take a moment to reflect on what change means to you personally. Is it the fear of losing familiarity or the anxiety of stepping into uncharted territory? By identifying the specific sources of your fear, you can begin to unravel their hold over you. Journaling can be an excellent tool for this process, allowing you to express your thoughts and feelings freely. As you write, you may discover that many of your fears are based on assumptions rather than reality, which can empower you to take the first step toward embracing change.

Mindfulness practices can also play a significant role in overcoming fear. Engaging in mindfulness allows you to stay present and grounded, helping to alleviate the stress that often accompanies thoughts of change. Simple techniques such as deep breathing, meditation, or gentle yoga can help calm your mind and body. By integrating these practices into your daily routine, you cultivate a sense of peace that enables you to approach change with a more balanced perspective. The more you focus on the present moment, the less power your fears will hold over you.

Building a support network can also be incredibly beneficial as you face the uncertainties of change. Connecting with friends, family, or a community group fosters a sense of belonging and reassurance. Sharing your feelings and experiences with others can not only provide comfort but also inspire you through their stories of resilience and transformation. Consider engaging with a life coach or joining a support group focused on wellness and personal growth. These connections remind you that you are not alone in your journey, and together, you can navigate the challenges that change brings.

Finally, it's essential to reframe your mindset about change. Instead of viewing it as a threat, see it as a chance to explore new opportunities and rediscover your passions. Embrace the idea that change can lead to personal growth, creativity, and a renewed sense of purpose. Set small, achievable goals that can help instill confidence as you begin to step outside your comfort zone. Each small success will build your self-esteem, allowing you to approach larger changes with a sense of empowerment. Remember, every step you take toward overcoming the fear of change brings you closer to a life filled with meaning and passion.

Chapter 8: Building Resilience

Coping with Life's Transitions

Coping with life's transitions is an essential aspect of embracing the golden years with grace and purpose. As we journey through life, we encounter a myriad of changes—retirement, loss of loved ones, health issues, or even simply the shift in daily routines. Each transition carries the potential for growth, and understanding how to navigate these changes can lead to profound personal development. Embracing the unknown with an open heart allows us to find new pathways to fulfillment, reminding us that age is not a limitation but an opportunity for renewal.

To cope effectively with transitions, it is vital to cultivate a mindset of resilience. This begins with acknowledging the emotions that arise during significant changes, whether they are feelings of sadness, anxiety, or confusion. Allowing ourselves to feel these emotions can be a powerful first step toward healing. Mindfulness practices can be particularly beneficial during these times. By focusing on the present moment, we can reduce stress and cultivate a sense of calm amidst the chaos. Simple breathing exercises, meditation, or even a gentle walk in nature can help ground us, enabling a clearer perspective on our circumstances.

Building a support network is another crucial aspect of coping with transitions. Engaging with friends, family, or community groups can provide a sense of belonging and comfort. Sharing our experiences with others who might be facing similar challenges fosters connection, allowing us to learn from each other's insights. Life coaching can also play an instrumental role in guiding individuals through these changes, offering tools and strategies to enhance self-esteem and confidence. A coach can help clarify goals and aspirations, making the transition feel less daunting and more like an exciting new chapter.

As we navigate through life's transitions, it's essential to rediscover our passions and purpose. This exploration can lead to a deeper understanding of who we are and what we want to achieve in this stage of life. Engaging in hobbies, volunteering, or pursuing new skills can reignite our sense of purpose and fulfillment. Spiritual life coaching can also offer valuable insights, helping us connect with our inner selves and explore the deeper meanings behind our experiences. This journey of self-discovery can transform transitions into opportunities for growth, creativity, and joy.

Ultimately, coping with life's transitions is about embracing change with an open heart and a spirit of curiosity. Each change brings with it the potential for new beginnings and fresh perspectives. By practicing mindfulness, seeking support, rediscovering passions, and cultivating resilience, we can not only cope with challenges but also thrive in the face of them. This period of life can be a remarkable time of transformation, where the lessons learned from past experiences become the foundation for a vibrant, purpose-driven future. Embrace these transitions as invitations to deepen your relationship with yourself and the world around you.

Strategies for Maintaining Positivity

As we journey through the later stages of life, maintaining a positive outlook becomes essential for our overall well-being and happiness. Embracing positivity not only enhances our daily experiences but also empowers us to navigate challenges with grace and resilience. One effective strategy for cultivating a positive mindset is the practice of gratitude. Taking time each day to reflect on the things we appreciate— whether it's a warm cup of tea, a friendly conversation, or simply the beauty of nature—can shift our focus from what we lack to what we have. Consider keeping a gratitude journal, where you can jot down three things you are thankful for each day. This simple act can serve as a powerful reminder of the abundance in your life.

Another vital strategy is engaging in meaningful social connections. As we age, it's not uncommon to feel isolated or disconnected. However, fostering relationships with family, friends, or community groups can significantly enhance our sense of purpose and joy. Make an effort to reach out to loved ones or join local clubs that align with your interests. Whether it's a book club, gardening group, or volunteering opportunity, these interactions can provide emotional support, inspiration, and a sense of belonging. Surrounding ourselves with positive influences nurtures our spirit and encourages us to maintain an optimistic perspective.

Mindfulness practices offer another avenue to sustain positivity. By cultivating a mindful approach to life, we can learn to appreciate the present moment and reduce stress. Activities such as meditation, deep breathing exercises, or gentle yoga can help center our thoughts and promote a sense of calm. Consider dedicating a few minutes each day to simply sit in silence, focus on your breath, and observe your thoughts without judgment. This practice not only enhances self-awareness but also helps to cultivate a more positive inner dialogue, enabling us to respond to challenges with clarity and compassion.

Spiritual exploration can also play a significant role in maintaining positivity. For many, connecting with a higher power or engaging in spiritual practices provides a deep sense of meaning and purpose. This can involve participating in a faith community, exploring philosophical teachings, or simply reflecting on your values and beliefs. Engaging in activities that resonate with your spiritual self can foster inner peace and provide a framework for understanding life's challenges. Embracing this aspect of our lives can inspire hope and positivity, reminding us of the greater purpose behind our experiences.

Lastly, pursuing passions and hobbies can invigorate our spirits and enhance our positivity. As we age, it's easy to let interests fall by the wayside, but engaging in activities that bring us joy can reignite our zest for life. Whether it's painting, gardening, writing, or learning a new skill, dedicating time to what you love can be incredibly fulfilling. Set aside regular time to explore these interests, and don't hesitate to try new things. Rediscovering passions can lead to new friendships, greater confidence, and a renewed sense of purpose, all of which contribute to a more positive outlook in the golden years of life.

Learning from Challenges

Learning from challenges is an essential aspect of personal growth, especially as we navigate the later stages of life. When faced with obstacles, it is natural to feel discouraged or overwhelmed. However, these challenges can serve as powerful teachers, guiding us toward greater self-awareness and deeper connections with our purpose. Embracing a mindset that views difficulties as opportunities for learning can transform our experiences and provide valuable insights into our passions and values.

In our journey through life, challenges often present themselves in various forms, whether they are health issues, the loss of loved ones, or the adjustments that come with retirement. Each situation can evoke a range of emotions, from sadness and frustration to fear and uncertainty. Acknowledging these feelings is the first step toward growth. By allowing ourselves to fully experience our emotions, we create space for reflection. This reflection helps us understand the lessons hidden within our struggles, enabling us to emerge stronger and more resilient.

One of the most significant benefits of reflecting on challenges is the opportunity to cultivate mindfulness. Mindfulness encourages us to remain present, allowing us to observe our thoughts and feelings without judgment. When we practice mindfulness during difficult times, we can better understand our reactions and choices. This awareness empowers us to respond thoughtfully rather than react impulsively, leading to healthier coping mechanisms and a greater sense of control over our lives. As we learn to navigate challenges with mindfulness, we also strengthen our self-esteem and confidence.

Moreover, challenges can illuminate our values and priorities, guiding us toward a more purposeful existence. When faced with adversity, we often reevaluate what truly matters to us. This process can reveal passions we may have set aside or aspects of our lives we wish to enhance. By identifying these values, we can align our actions with our intentions, creating a life that is more fulfilling and meaningful. It's an opportunity to redefine our goals, seek new passions, and engage in activities that resonate with our true selves.

In conclusion, learning from challenges is a vital component of our personal development, especially in our later years. By reframing our experiences as opportunities for growth and reflection, we can cultivate a positive mindset that empowers us to embrace change. With each challenge we face, we have the chance to deepen our understanding of ourselves and our purpose. As we embark on this journey of discovery, let us remember that every obstacle can lead to greater wisdom and a renewed sense of passion for life. Embrace the lessons that come your way, and allow them to guide you toward a more vibrant and fulfilling existence.

Chapter 9: Nurturing Relationships

The Role of Community and Connection

The journey of life is often enriched by the connections we forge within our communities. As we age, the significance of these relationships becomes even more pronounced. Community and connection serve not only as sources of support but also as catalysts for personal growth, fostering a sense of belonging that is essential for our emotional and mental well-being. Engaging with others can help us rediscover passions, nurture our self-esteem, and instill a renewed purpose in life. The companionship found in shared experiences can illuminate paths we may not have considered, guiding us toward fulfilling our deepest desires.

In this stage of life, it's vital to recognize that everyone has valuable contributions to make. Participating in community activities, whether through volunteering, joining clubs, or attending local events, allows individuals to showcase their unique skills and insights. This engagement not only bolsters one's confidence but also cultivates a sense of purpose. Each interaction becomes an opportunity for reflection, helping us understand our place in the world and how we can positively impact those around us. By focusing on the strengths we possess, we can foster self-esteem and create a ripple effect that inspires others to do the same.

Mindfulness plays a crucial role in enhancing our connections. Being present in our interactions allows us to truly listen and engage with others, deepening our relationships. Mindful communication encourages openness and understanding, breaking down barriers that may have been built over the years. As we practice mindfulness, we cultivate an environment where mutual support thrives. This nurturing space can lead to the exploration of new ideas and insights, enriching our own lives while helping others to flourish. The beauty of connection lies in its mutuality—by uplifting others, we inevitably uplift ourselves.

Spirituality often intertwines with community, offering a profound sense of interconnectedness. Many find that exploring spiritual practices within a group setting fosters a deeper understanding of themselves and their purpose. Whether through meditation circles, faith-based gatherings, or spiritual retreats, these shared experiences can ignite a passion for living with intention. They create a sanctuary where individuals can reflect on their journeys and the roles they play within a larger narrative. This exploration can lead to transformations that reverberate through every aspect of life, enhancing well-being and igniting a sense of passion for the future.

Ultimately, embracing the role of community and connection allows us to navigate the later stages of life with joy and purpose. As we invest in relationships and engage with others, we open ourselves to new experiences and opportunities for growth. The wisdom gained over the years becomes a beacon for those who seek guidance, while also reminding us that we are never truly alone. By fostering connections, we discover not only the richness of life but also the profound impact we can have on others, creating a legacy of compassion and inspiration that endures.

Effective Communication Skills

Effective communication skills are essential tools that can enhance our connections with others, especially as we navigate the beautiful complexities of life after 60. At this stage, many of us seek deeper relationships and a greater understanding of ourselves and our surroundings. By honing our communication skills, we can express our thoughts and feelings more clearly, allowing us to engage more meaningfully with friends, family, and even new acquaintances. This chapter will explore the vital components of effective communication and how they can enrich our lives during this transformative period.

One fundamental aspect of effective communication is active listening. This means not only hearing the words spoken by someone else but also fully engaging with their message. For many, life after 60 brings with it a wealth of experiences and stories worth sharing. By practicing active listening, we show respect and genuine interest in others, which fosters trust and deeper connections. Simple techniques such as maintaining eye contact, nodding in acknowledgment, and asking follow-up questions can significantly enhance our conversations. Remember, every interaction is an opportunity to learn and grow, both for ourselves and those around us.

Expressing ourselves clearly and confidently is another critical skill in effective communication. As we age, we may sometimes find it challenging to articulate our thoughts due to self-doubt or the fear of being misunderstood. Yet, embracing our life experiences gives us a unique perspective that deserves to be shared. Practicing self-affirmation can bolster our confidence, reminding us that our voices matter. It may be helpful to engage in activities such as journaling or joining discussion groups, where we can articulate our ideas in a supportive environment. As we become more comfortable sharing our truths, we inspire others to do the same.

Non-verbal communication also plays a crucial role in how we connect with others. Our body language, facial expressions, and tone of voice all convey messages that can either enhance or undermine our spoken words. Being mindful of these elements can significantly improve our interactions. For example, a warm smile or an open posture can invite others to approach us, while a closed stance or lack of eye contact may create barriers. By becoming aware of our non-verbal cues, we can convey warmth, openness, and sincerity, which are essential components of effective communication.

Finally, cultivating empathy is a cornerstone of effective communication. As we reflect on our life experiences, we gain insights into the struggles and joys of others. By approaching conversations with empathy, we create a safe space for others to express themselves. This fosters an environment where vulnerability is welcomed, and deeper connections can flourish. Engaging in mindfulness practices can enhance our ability to empathize, helping us to be present and attuned to the emotions of those around us. With each meaningful conversation, we not only discover more about ourselves but also contribute to a collective narrative that enriches our communities and our lives.

In embracing these effective communication skills, we open doors to new relationships, experiences, and personal growth. Life after 60 is an exciting chapter filled with opportunities to connect, reflect, and rediscover ourselves. By committing to enhance our communication abilities, we not only elevate our own lives but also uplift those of others, creating a ripple effect of understanding and compassion in the world around us.

Building New Friendships

Building new friendships in your later years can be a transformative experience, offering fresh perspectives and enriching your life in ways you may not have anticipated. As we age, it is natural for some friendships to fade due to various life changes like relocation, retirement, or the passing of loved ones. Embracing this transition as an opportunity to forge new connections can reignite your sense of purpose and passion. Remember, friendship is not just a luxury; it is a vital component of emotional and mental well-being that can enhance your overall health.

The first step in building new friendships involves stepping out of your comfort zone. This can feel daunting, but it is essential to remember that many others are also seeking connection. Consider joining community groups, participating in local classes, or engaging in volunteer opportunities that align with your interests. These environments are ripe for meeting like-minded individuals who share your passions. Additionally, technology has made it easier than ever to connect. Online platforms and social media can help you find clubs or groups, allowing for meaningful interactions from the comfort of your home.

As you seek new friendships, focus on developing your self-confidence. Often, the fear of rejection can hold us back from reaching out to others. Recognize that your life experiences and wisdom are valuable assets that can attract potential friends. Practice self-affirmation by reminding yourself of your strengths and the unique qualities you bring to a relationship. Engaging in activities that boost your self-esteem, such as taking up a new hobby or achieving personal goals, can empower you to approach others with a sense of assurance and openness.

Mindfulness can also play a critical role in building new friendships. By being present in your interactions and actively listening to others, you can cultivate deeper connections. Practice being curious about the people you meet; ask questions and show genuine interest in their stories. This not only helps you learn about them but also fosters a sense of belonging and mutual understanding. Remember that friendships blossom when there is a foundation of trust and authenticity, and being fully engaged in conversations will highlight your desire to connect.

Lastly, embrace the idea that friendship is a two-way street that requires effort and nurturing. Be proactive in maintaining your new connections by reaching out regularly, suggesting meet-ups, or even sharing experiences that you both enjoy. The beauty of building new friendships lies in the shared journey of discovery, laughter, and support. With each new relationship, you create opportunities to learn more about yourself while enriching the lives of others. As you embark on this journey of creating new friendships, remember that the best is yet to come, and the connections you make can add immeasurable joy and purpose to your life.

Chapter 10: Celebrating Your Journey

Reflecting on Growth and Progress

Reflecting on growth and progress is a vital aspect of the journey we embark upon as we age. For many, the years beyond sixty are not merely a time of looking back, but rather an opportunity to assess how far we have come and what we have learned along the way. This reflection allows us to celebrate our achievements, no matter how small, and recognize the resilience we have developed throughout our lives. Embracing this perspective can empower us to approach our later years with renewed enthusiasm and a deeper understanding of our purpose.

As we reflect on our lives, it's essential to acknowledge the various experiences that have shaped us. Each challenge faced, every joy celebrated, and all the relationships we've nurtured contribute to our growth. Whether it was navigating a career, raising a family, or pursuing personal passions, these experiences have equipped us with unique insights that can guide our future endeavors. Taking the time to document these milestones, perhaps through journaling or storytelling, can serve as a powerful reminder of our capabilities and the wisdom we've accumulated.

Mindfulness plays a crucial role in this reflective process. By being present in the moment, we can more effectively appreciate our past while remaining open to future possibilities. Mindful reflection encourages us to embrace our emotions—both the joyous and the difficult—allowing us to process our experiences fully. This practice not only enhances our emotional well-being but also cultivates a deeper sense of gratitude for the life we have lived and the lessons we have learned.

Moreover, growth is not confined to personal achievements; it encompasses our relationships with others and the impact we have on the world around us. Engaging in community activities, volunteering, or mentoring younger generations can provide profound fulfillment and a sense of purpose. These connections enrich our lives and remind us that our experiences are valuable and can inspire others. Reflecting on how we have contributed to the lives of others helps us realize that our journey is interwoven with the stories of those we encounter, fostering a sense of belonging and significance.

In conclusion, reflecting on growth and progress after sixty is not just an exercise in nostalgia; it is a powerful tool for self-discovery and empowerment. By embracing our past, practicing mindfulness, and recognizing the impact we have on others, we can forge a path filled with purpose and passion. Each day presents an opportunity to continue this journey of growth, allowing us to step into our later years with confidence and a renewed sense of direction. As we reflect, let us celebrate the beautiful tapestry of our lives and look forward to the chapters yet to be written.

Sharing Your Story with Others

Sharing your story with others is an empowering act that can foster connection, healing, and understanding. For many, the experiences and lessons learned over a lifetime hold immense value, not only for ourselves but also for those around us. As you embark on this journey of purposeful reflection, consider the ways in which articulating your narrative can enrich your life and the lives of others. This sharing is not merely an exercise in storytelling; it is a powerful opportunity to inspire, teach, and build relationships that resonate with authenticity and warmth.

Engaging in storytelling encourages self-reflection and introspection, vital components of wellness coaching. By recounting your own experiences, you can identify patterns and insights that may have gone unnoticed. This process can illuminate your strengths, highlight areas for growth, and deepen your understanding of what truly matters to you. As you reflect on your journey, remember that vulnerability is a strength. Sharing your challenges and triumphs can resonate with others who may be experiencing similar struggles, creating a sense of community and support.

In the realm of confidence and self-esteem coaching, sharing your story can significantly boost your self-worth. When you recount your experiences, you validate your own life's journey, recognizing the courage it took to navigate various challenges. This acknowledgment not only reinforces your self-esteem but can also inspire others to embrace their narratives. The simple act of expressing your thoughts and feelings can break down barriers of isolation, fostering a sense of belonging and encouraging others to share their own stories.

Mindfulness and stress management coaching emphasize the importance of being present in the moment, and storytelling can be a form of mindfulness practice. When you share your story, you engage fully in the act of communication, allowing yourself to be vulnerable and authentic. This presence can lead to profound insights and a greater appreciation for the richness of your life experiences. Moreover, listening to others' stories can deepen your empathy and understanding, creating a reciprocal exchange that enhances emotional well-being for both parties.

Lastly, sharing your story is a vital aspect of spiritual life coaching and discovering your purpose. Your narrative is a tapestry of experiences that reflects your values, beliefs, and passions. By articulating your journey, you can uncover themes that guide you toward your true purpose. Each story shared is a step toward self-discovery and fulfillment. Embrace the opportunity to connect with others through your story, and you may find that in the process, you not only inspire them but also uncover new layers of meaning and passion within yourself.

Looking Ahead with Hope and Joy

Looking ahead with hope and joy is a powerful mindset that can transform the way we perceive our later years. As we gather the wisdom of our experiences, it becomes essential to embrace the opportunities that lie ahead. This is a time to reflect on past achievements, recognizing that each moment has contributed to the tapestry of our lives. By focusing on what is yet to come, we can cultivate a sense of excitement and possibility, reminding ourselves that life continues to unfold with new adventures, relationships, and passions waiting to be discovered.

In the journey of life, our perspective shapes our experiences. Choosing to see the world through a lens of hope allows us to approach each day with renewed energy and enthusiasm. This practice encourages us not only to set new goals but also to celebrate the small victories along the way. Whether it's pursuing a hobby that brings joy, volunteering for a cause close to our hearts, or simply enjoying the beauty of each day, we can infuse our lives with purpose and meaning. Each step forward can reignite our confidence and self-esteem, reminding us of our inherent value and capacity for growth.

Mindfulness plays a crucial role in fostering hope and joy. By being present in the moment, we can appreciate the richness of our experiences without being weighed down by regrets or fears about the future. Engaging in mindfulness practices—such as meditation, deep breathing, or even mindful walking—can help us center ourselves, reducing stress and opening our hearts to gratitude. This state of awareness allows us to connect with our inner selves, enabling us to recognize what truly brings us joy and fulfillment. In this way, we can align our actions with our values, creating a life that resonates with our deepest passions.

Spiritual exploration also offers a pathway to hope and joy. Many individuals find comfort and inspiration in spiritual teachings, which can provide guidance in navigating the complexities of life after sixty. Whether through traditional religious practices or personal spiritual journeys, connecting with something greater than ourselves can foster a sense of belonging and purpose. Engaging in discussions about spirituality with like-minded individuals can deepen our understanding and encourage us to embrace the unknown with courage and optimism.

As we look ahead, it is vital to remember that the greatest chapters of our lives are still unwritten. Each day presents a blank canvas for us to paint our dreams, aspirations, and joys. With a commitment to personal growth and a willingness to explore new possibilities, we can approach the future with an open heart and mind. Let us nurture our passions, cultivate meaningful relationships, and live with intention, knowing that the joy we seek is often found in the journey itself. Embrace this beautiful season of life with hope, and let it inspire us to create a legacy of love, laughter, and purpose.

Chapter 11: Resources for Continued Growth

Recommended Reading and Activities

In the journey of discovering meaning and passion after 60, engaging with thoughtful literature can be a transformative experience. This subchapter, "Recommended Reading and Activities," aims to guide you toward resources that not only inspire but also enrich your understanding of yourself and the world around you. Books that explore themes of resilience, self-discovery, and mindfulness can provide valuable insights, encouraging you to reflect on your life experiences and aspirations. Titles such as "The Gifts of Imperfection" by Brené Brown and "The Art of Happiness" by the Dalai Lama offer profound wisdom that resonates deeply, fostering a sense of connection and purpose.

In addition to reading, incorporating activities that promote self-reflection can significantly enhance your journey. Journaling is a powerful tool that allows you to articulate your thoughts and feelings, helping you to clarify your goals and values. Set aside time each week to write about your experiences, aspirations, and the lessons you've learned. This practice not only boosts self-awareness but also cultivates a deeper understanding of what truly matters to you. Consider prompts such as "What brings me joy?" or "What legacy do I wish to create?" to stimulate your reflections.

Mindfulness practices, such as meditation and yoga, can further enrich your exploration of purpose and passion. These activities encourage you to be present in the moment, reducing stress and fostering a sense of inner peace. Many resources are available, including guided meditation apps, local classes, or online workshops that cater specifically to older adults. Embracing mindfulness not only enhances your overall well-being but also opens the door to greater self-acceptance and appreciation for the present moment, vital components in the quest for a meaningful life.

Exploring new interests or revisiting old hobbies can also reignite your passion for life. Whether it's painting, gardening, or learning a musical instrument, engaging in creative activities can provide a refreshing outlet for self-expression. Joining a local club or class can connect you with like-minded individuals, fostering a sense of community and belonging. These shared experiences not only enhance your skills but also create opportunities for new friendships, reminding you that it's never too late to pursue your passions.

Lastly, consider seeking out life coaching or workshops that focus on confidence-building and purpose discovery. Many organizations offer programs tailored for older adults, focusing on personal growth and fulfillment. These resources provide a supportive environment where you can explore your aspirations, redefine your goals, and gain practical strategies for achieving them. Remember, the journey of self-discovery is ongoing, and by engaging with recommended readings and activities, you are taking vital steps toward a life filled with meaning and passion. Embrace this exciting chapter with an open heart and a curious mind; the best is yet to come.

Finding the Right Coaching Support

Finding the right coaching support can be a transformative journey, especially after reaching the milestone of 60. At this stage of life, many individuals seek to rediscover their passions, improve their well-being, and cultivate a deeper sense of purpose. Engaging with a coach can provide the guidance and encouragement needed to navigate this exciting phase. However, selecting the right coach is crucial to ensure that your personal goals are met in a way that resonates with your unique experiences and aspirations.

Begin by reflecting on what you hope to achieve through coaching. Are you looking to improve your health and wellness? Perhaps you want to bolster your self-esteem or learn how to manage stress effectively. Identifying your primary objectives will help you narrow down the type of coaching support that aligns with your needs. Different coaches specialize in various areas, such as life coaching, wellness, mindfulness, or spiritual guidance. Understanding your specific goals will empower you to seek out a coach who can best support your journey.

Once you have clarity on your goals, research potential coaches in your area or online. Look for professionals who have experience working with individuals over 60, as they will be more attuned to the unique challenges and opportunities this demographic faces. Read their biographies, testimonials, and any available reviews to gauge their expertise and approach. Don't hesitate to reach out and ask questions about their methods and philosophies. A personal connection is essential in coaching; you should feel comfortable and understood by your coach.

As you begin to interview potential coaches, pay attention to how they communicate and whether they listen actively to your concerns. A good coach will create a safe space for reflection and exploration, allowing you to delve into your thoughts and feelings without judgment. Look for someone who encourages you to set achievable goals and celebrates your successes, no matter how small. The right coach will not only offer guidance but also empower you to take ownership of your journey, fostering your confidence and resilience.

Finally, trust your instincts when making your choice. The coaching relationship is deeply personal, and finding someone who resonates with you on a fundamental level can make all the difference. Once you find the right coach, embrace the process with an open mind and heart. This partnership can lead to profound insights, renewed energy, and a clearer sense of purpose, making your journey after 60 not just fulfilling but also deeply enriching. Remember, it's never too late to pursue your passions and discover the life you truly want to live.

Online Communities for Connection

In today's digital age, online communities have emerged as vibrant spaces for connection, especially for those over 60 seeking to rediscover their purpose and passion. These communities offer an opportunity to engage with like-minded individuals who share similar interests, experiences, and aspirations. For anyone navigating the complexities of life after retirement, these virtual gatherings can provide a sense of belonging and support that enriches personal growth and well-being.

Joining an online community tailored to life coaching or wellness can significantly enhance your journey toward self-discovery. These platforms often host discussions, workshops, and resources that encourage members to explore their goals and passions. Whether you're looking to foster better health, improve your confidence and self-esteem, or learn mindfulness techniques, these groups offer invaluable tools and insights. Engaging actively in such environments can inspire you to take meaningful steps toward the life you envision for yourself.

Moreover, online communities are excellent venues for practicing mindfulness and stress management.

They provide a safe space to share experiences and challenges while learning from others who have faced similar hurdles. Participating in guided meditations, stress-relief exercises, or simply sharing your thoughts can help cultivate a sense of calm and clarity. The collective wisdom found in these communities often leads to new coping strategies and a renewed sense of purpose, reminding you that you are not alone on this journey.

Spiritual life coaching is another niche that thrives within online communities. These spaces encourage introspection and exploration of what spirituality means to you. By connecting with others who are also seeking deeper meaning, you can engage in discussions about your beliefs, values, and experiences. Sharing your journey with a supportive network can lead to profound insights, helping you to align your daily actions with your spiritual aspirations. This connection can be a powerful catalyst for personal transformation.

Finally, the act of connecting with others online fosters a sense of community that can be invigorating and uplifting. As you share your stories, celebrate your achievements, and learn from each other, you create a rich tapestry of support and encouragement. These relationships can motivate you to pursue your passions with renewed vigor and enthusiasm. Remember, the journey of discovering your purpose and passion is not meant to be traveled alone. Embrace the resources and connections available in online communities, and allow them to guide you toward a fulfilling and meaningful life after 60.

Chapter 12: Your Next Chapter

Embracing the Future with Open Arms

Embracing the future with open arms is a powerful mindset that can transform the way we perceive the later stages of our lives. As we age, it is natural to reflect on the past and consider what lies ahead. However, this period can also be an opportunity for renewal and growth. When we approach the future with optimism and curiosity, we open ourselves to new possibilities. This chapter encourages you to shift your perspective, embracing each day as a chance to explore, learn, and connect with the world around you.

The journey of self-discovery does not end at sixty; in fact, it can be just beginning. Life coaching can play a vital role in this journey, helping you to identify your values, passions, and goals. Through guided reflection and support, you can uncover what truly matters to you. This process can lead to a sense of purpose that fuels your days with excitement and intention. By setting new objectives, whether they are small or grand, you can find fulfillment and motivation that revitalizes your spirit.

Wellness and health coaching can also be invaluable as you navigate this exciting new chapter. Prioritizing your physical well-being not only enhances your vitality but also boosts your mental and emotional health. Simple changes in your daily routine, such as incorporating regular exercise, balanced nutrition, and mindfulness practices, can significantly impact your overall quality of life. Embracing the future means nurturing your body and mind, allowing you to engage fully in the experiences that await you.

Confidence and self-esteem coaching is equally essential as you embrace this new phase of life. Many individuals may struggle with feelings of uncertainty as they transition into retirement or face the loss of loved ones. However, this is your time to rediscover your strengths and capabilities. By fostering self-compassion and resilience, you can build a strong foundation of confidence that enables you to face challenges head-on. Remember that your past achievements and experiences have equipped you with valuable skills that can be applied to new endeavors.

Finally, spiritual life coaching can provide a profound sense of connection and purpose in your later years. Engaging in practices that nurture your spirit, such as meditation, reflection, or community involvement, can deepen your understanding of yourself and your place in the world. As you embrace the future, consider how you can contribute to something greater than yourself. Whether through volunteering, mentoring, or sharing your wisdom, your life experiences can inspire others and create a ripple effect of positivity. By welcoming the future with open arms, you not only enrich your own life but also uplift those around you, creating a legacy of love, purpose, and passion.

Continuing the Journey of Discovery

Continuing the journey of discovery after sixty is a vital and exhilarating chapter in life. As we age, the opportunities for personal growth and self-exploration expand rather than diminish. Embracing this stage with curiosity and an open heart allows us to redefine our purpose and uncover passions that may have been set aside during the busyness of earlier years. The wisdom acquired over decades can serve as a guiding light, illuminating pathways to new experiences and deeper understanding of ourselves.

Engaging in life coaching can be an invaluable tool during this transformative period. A skilled coach can help you identify your goals and aspirations, encouraging you to dream big and think beyond conventional boundaries. This collaborative relationship fosters accountability and motivation, empowering you to take actionable steps toward your desired future. By focusing on your strengths and values, you can create a personalized roadmap that reflects what truly matters to you, paving the way for meaningful exploration.

Wellness and health coaching play a crucial role in this journey, emphasizing the importance of physical, mental, and emotional well-being. By prioritizing a holistic approach to health, you can cultivate energy and vitality, enabling you to pursue passions with vigor. Small, sustainable changes in your daily routine can lead to significant improvements in your quality of life. Whether it's adopting a new exercise regimen, exploring nutritious cooking, or practicing relaxation techniques, each step taken is a testament to your commitment to living fully and vibrantly.

Confidence and self-esteem coaching can also be transformative in this stage of life. As we age, societal narratives may challenge our self-worth, making it essential to nurture a positive self-image. Through guided reflection and support, you can challenge limiting beliefs and celebrate your unique contributions to the world. Embracing your individuality allows you to approach new challenges with renewed confidence, whether it's picking up a new hobby, volunteering, or even starting a new business venture.

Mindfulness and spiritual life coaching can deepen your connection to yourself and the world around you. Practicing mindfulness fosters a sense of presence and awareness, allowing you to appreciate the beauty in everyday moments. Spiritual coaching encourages you to explore your beliefs, values, and the essence of your existence. This exploration can provide a profound sense of peace and purpose, guiding you towards a life that resonates with authenticity. As you continue your journey of discovery, remember that it is never too late to embrace new adventures, cultivate passions, and live a life filled with meaning and joy.

Leaving a Legacy of Purpose and Passion

Leaving a legacy of purpose and passion is a profound way to transition into the later stages of life, especially after 60. This chapter invites you to reflect on the unique gifts you possess and how you can share them with the world. At this stage of life, many find themselves yearning for a deeper connection to their own purpose. It is not merely about what you will leave behind, but rather how you can continue to impact those around you through your experiences, wisdom, and passion.

As you embark on this journey of self-discovery, consider what truly ignites your spirit. What activities make you feel alive? What causes stir your passion? Engaging in these reflections not only clarifies your purpose but also helps you identify the legacy you wish to create. Connecting with your passions can provide a sense of fulfillment that transcends age. Whether it's through mentoring younger generations, volunteering for causes close to your heart, or even sharing your life stories, your experiences hold the power to inspire and motivate others.

In this chapter, we also explore the importance of wellness and health in maintaining the energy necessary to pursue your passions. Embracing a holistic approach to health—encompassing physical, emotional, and spiritual well-being—enables you to cultivate resilience and vitality. Mindfulness practices, stress management techniques, and a focus on self-care can significantly enhance your quality of life, allowing you to engage fully in your endeavors. Remember, your well-being is a vital component of the legacy you leave; nurturing yourself creates a strong foundation for sharing your passions with the world.

Confidence and self-esteem play crucial roles in how you express your purpose. Many individuals may grapple with doubts about their worthiness or the impact they can have at this stage in life. It's essential to acknowledge and challenge these limiting beliefs. Through self-reflection and supportive coaching, you can build the confidence needed to step into your legacy with pride. Embrace the notion that your voice matters, your experiences are valuable, and your contributions can make a difference, no matter how small they may seem.

Ultimately, leaving a legacy of purpose and passion involves embracing your journey with an open heart and mind. As you reflect on what you want to impart to future generations, think about the values you hold dear and the lessons you've learned. Your life story is a tapestry woven with rich experiences, and by sharing it, you not only celebrate your own journey but also empower others to find their own paths. This chapter encourages you to take bold steps toward living a life that reflects your true essence, ensuring that your legacy continues to inspire long after you've moved on.

Acknowledgement

The information presented in this book is intended solely for informational purposes and should not be used for medical, therapeutic, or educational purposes. The exercises and advice provided within are to be followed and undertaken by the reader with full responsibility and common sense. The author and publishers are not liable for any misuse or misinterpretation of the information contained in this book. Readers are encouraged to consult qualified professionals for any specific concerns or issues related to their personal situation. The author and publishers make no warranties regarding the accuracy or completeness of the information provided and accept no liability for any damages resulting from its use. The images and illustrations are included to enhance the reading experience, and the artist assumes no responsibility for any discomfort or harm that may result to the reader.

Author Biography on Amazon Books